The Interrupted Life
LESSONS FROM JONAH

PRISCILLA SHIRER

LifeWay Press®. Nashville, Tennessee

Published by LifeWay Press®
© 2010 Priscilla Shirer

ISBN 9781415869345
Item 005325612

Dewey Decimal Classification: 224.02
Subject Heading: BIBLE. OT. JONAH—STUDY\GOD\WILL\
JONAH, PROPHET

Unless otherwise indicated, Scripture quotations are from the
New American Standard Bible copyright © 1960, 1962, 1963,
1968, 1971, 1973, 1975, 1995 by the Lockman Foundation.
Used by permission *(www.lockman.org)*. Scripture quotations
marked NIV are from the Holy Bible, New International Version,
copyright © 1973, 1978, 1984 by International Bible Society.

To order additional copies of this resource:
Write LifeWay Church Resources Customer Service;
One LifeWay Plaza; Nashville, TN 37234-0113;
fax order to (615) 251-5933; phone (800) 458-2772;
order online at *www.lifeway.com;* e-mail *orderentry@lifeway.com;*
or visit the LifeWay Christian Store serving you.

Printed in the United States of America

Leadership and Adult Publishing
Lifeway Church Resources
One LifeWay Plaza
Nashville, TN 37234-0175

CONTENTS

INTERRUPTIONS 4

CHAPTER 1 10
Take Two

CHAPTER 2 20
Second Chances

CHAPTER 3 32
Shortcuts

CHAPTER 4 40
Moving Forward

CHAPTER 5 48
Making Good & Making Amends

CONCLUSION 55

ABOUT THE AUTHOR. 60

INTERRUPTIONS

You know how it feels, right? You've got one free hour to do as you please and something happens causing that beloved 60 minutes to disappear like a forgotten dream. Frustrating. Or, you've mapped out a plan for your day and a traffic jam derails your whole schedule. Irritating, isn't it?

What if it's not just that all-important hour or even a particularly strategic day that's interrupted; what if it's your whole life? You planned one thing for this season, and yet your current situation looks nothing like what you had in mind. Someone or something tampered with your ambitions, goals, and dreams. The yellow-brick road of life veered off in some unexpected direction.

You're not the only one who can relate. Jonah knows exactly how you feel. As a prophet to the Northern Kingdom of Israel, Jonah's priorities included hearing from God and declaring God's messages to His people. The prophet lived in a time of economic prosperity as Israel regained lost territories, just as Jonah said they would, and achieved its most prosperous time since Solomon. While we know little of Jonah's life prior to the events in the book, we do know Jonah had foretold good things for Israel that came to pass. As a result, the prophet was likely popular, highly respected, and appreciated. Life was good.

In Jonah 1:1, however, "The word of the LORD" came to the prophet—not in the form of good news for the inhabitants of Israel but as a warning and call to repentance for Gentiles, specifically the people of pagan Nineveh who had a reputation for brutality. Jonah had spent his life declaring good things for Israel, and now he was being sent to their enemies. This was not what he'd expected. For Jonah this call, this interruption, held little appeal.

Interrupted lives—probably an accurate descriptor for points in all of our journeys, don't you think? We all chart out a tidy path of goals

5

for our lives. I certainly had. Without even realizing it, I'd taken my life by the helm and asked God to conform to my flimsy timetable and arrangements.

This was never clearer than when baby Jude, our third spectacular yet surprising gift from God, began growing in my tummy. We were shocked at the prospect of life with a newborn ... again. Yet through this new adventure, God began to expose my tendency to cling to my own plans instead of embracing His purposes for me, even when they differ from what I deem suited for my abilities.

Your interruptions may differ from mine. In fact, I suspect they do. Life's far too individual and unexpected to treat us all the same. Maybe you face looming retirement with a diminishing nest egg in a crumbling economy. Perhaps you're staring down another year of singleness when you long for marriage. Maybe your spouse's revealed secret threatens your security or a new baby or two will soon arrive, requiring all the attention that little ones do. You might find yourself overwhelmed by a burst of business success far beyond your capacity to manage or feel God redirecting you into ministry that means abandoning a lucrative corporate career. You may even struggle to overcome yet another heartbreaking year of battling infertility or coming to grips with a tragic loss. No matter how unique our situations, we've clearly been thrust into something we weren't planning.

Without doubt interruptions can be difficult to manage, and we often interpret them—at least at first—as maddening annoyances. But no matter the specifics, interruptions might well open the door to a holy privilege.

When we signed up to follow Christ, we agreed to be open to divine intervention—God interruptions. While His "call" might not always be convenient or easy, responding to it should not just be a duty but our joy. God graciously gives divine interventions to His children, providing us with opportunities to partner in His purposes. He has kingdom purposes and plans, and He wants to include us in their unfolding.

Jonah didn't see the call to go to Nineveh as a privilege; instead, he ran from it, tried to turn down the interruption, and in doing so attempted to rewrite God's plan for his life. What did his efforts earn him? An unpleasant stay in a fish.

When, however, Jonah was given a miraculous second chance, he finally yielded to the Lord. When he did, Jonah's ordinary existence became extraordinary. Not only did the prophet spark what some scholars call the greatest revival in human history but as a result of the mission he was mentioned in the New Testament by Jesus. The prophet's story really began not in a storm or when he found himself spat out on the shore but when he yielded to God's divine interruption and made an eternal imprint on humanity.

Maybe you've been running from God's clear direction for your life. Maybe you initially refused to follow His plan or you've engaged but only begrudgingly. I encourage you to consider that maybe, just maybe, this interruption is a divinely sealed invitation to be a part of something

unfathomably spectacular. God wants to shape
and use your life in amazing ways. Even if you've
balked or complained or run away from Him in the
past, know that He extends you a second chance to
partner with Him.

God's call on your life, what He's asking you
to surrender to right now in this season, means
that He has chosen you above anyone else to do
what He's asking. You are the one He singled out
as His partner for a particular project. Whether
it's parenting a special needs child, starting a Bible
study, or even, like Jonah, reaching out to those
who you'd rather avoid, He's purposefully given
you the high honor of being the one He deemed
suited for a task with heavenly implications.

A supernatural outcome waits on the horizon
for anyone who chooses to partner with God. So go
ahead, sit on the edge of your seat in anticipation.
Accept that interruption for the gift that it is.

God offers you a chance to write a story
of eternal significance and it all begins ... with
an interruption.

Chapter 1
TAKE TWO

*Forgiveness of past sins qualifies
us for present service.*

Many believe that one big mess-up in a Christian's life forever disqualifies them from effectively serving God, but this misunderstanding ignores a beautiful reality: Forgiveness of past sins qualifies us for present service.

The most humbling times in my life are undoubtedly those when I am on a platform teaching God's people. With Bible perched under my arm, notes tucked inside, heart palpitating in my chest, and eyes scanning the crowd, I ask the audience to bow for a quick prayer before the message begins. I'm praying not only because I need God's empowerment but because I need a minute to gain my composure.

You see, I'm stunned. Every time I'm getting ready to open God's Word and teach from it, I'm in complete disbelief. Why He didn't relegate me to the proverbial shelf long ago, I'll never know.

Like Jonah, in so many moments of rebellion, I've chosen a lifestyle out of sync with God's will for me. Yet for some odd reason He still lets me partner with Him.

I handle this position with care. I'm too shocked to do otherwise.

Is there something God has allowed in your life, some type of beauty-for-ashes miracle He has allowed, the sight of which causes you to simply stand back, mouth agape in wonder, and stare? How can we not take time to relish the wonder of God's mercy?

A constant tension plagues the human existence. It begins the moment we are born: Our flesh wants to go one way when God wants to lead us in another direction. It's evident we see this as our sin nature battles against God's standards, but we also find it in our tendency to make choices that conflict with His plans. Throughout our lives our wills battle God's will. Our ambitions try to squeeze out His ambitions for us. Our goals for ourselves fall short of His goals for us. While it's tempting to think that living for God might prove impossible, every major spiritual player in the Bible dealt with this tension between our will and God's and most—though often after a failure or two—eventually got it right.

In Jonah 3:1-2 the prophet found himself washed up on a beach where he received a fresh opportunity to follow God's direction: "Now the word of the LORD came to Jonah the second time, saying, 'Arise, go to Nineveh.' " Hear that again: "The word of the LORD came … the second time." What follows is a stunning and fantastic reminder of the mercy and grace available to all those who have messed up and need to know that they aren't all washed up: Jonah's relationship with God was restored, and as a result of his ministry, Nineveh underwent drastic revival.

Most biblical people who made a lasting mark in Christianity had a point where they stood at a crossroad. They had to decide to yield to divine intervention at the cost of their own plans or continue their own path instead. From Noah's call to build an unfamiliar object called an ark to Peter's being told to go to the house of a Gentile named Cornelius, any person God used mightily for His glory both began and continued his or her journey with divine interruptions. As they yielded to God's purposes, they unknowingly wrote life stories that made a mark on history. Many of these individuals, however, first tried to control their own destinies before wisely and fully submitting to God's plans. I call their stories second-chance miracles.

First, consider Aaron's life. Aaron is known mostly as Moses' brother. He played second fiddle to Moses, serving as his mouthpiece when he went to stand before Pharaoh. In the wilderness, when the Israelites waged war against the Amalekites, Aaron wasn't in the trenches of battle making a name for himself but standing beside his brother, holding up his hands in prayer (Ex. 17:12). Aaron seemed to have a hard time coming out from underneath the shadow of his older sibling. Yet he had a high calling on his life by God as well.

God set Aaron apart to officiate in the tabernacle. As the high priest, he served as the mediator between God and His chosen people. He had the privilege of entering the most holy place and experiencing the delight of God's presence in a way few ever would. Even Aaron's garments were specifically prepared to distinguish him and to ascribe dignity to his role within the community of faith.

While Moses was on Mount Sinai receiving instructions from God for the making of Aaron's garment and his consecration, things began to unravel (Ex. 24:15-18; 28). At this moment of divine dialogue between Moses and Yahweh, a great injustice was occurring at the foot of the mountain: Aaron was crafting an idol in the shape of a calf, encouraging the people to revere it as the god who had led them out of Egypt.

Can you imagine Moses' disbelief at Aaron's actions when he stepped foot off Sinai? While Moses may have been shocked, God was not. Even while He was giving instructions to Moses,

God was fully aware of His chosen vessel staging a rebellion against Him. Yet Aaron was given a second chance. He was still allowed to serve as Israel's first high priest.

Sarah too needed more than one opportunity to walk faithfully with God. Sarah was Abraham's wife. God gave her a promise: She would have a son and become the mother of an entire nation of people. Abraham and Sarah had a track record of trusting God. When God told Abraham to leave Ur and go to an unspecified place, they did it with no questions asked. But when God said Sarah would become pregnant, she laughed heartily, considering her age and record of infertility. Ultimately, she knew that neither were hurdles too big for God to overcome, but after 10 years of waiting to see proof of God's promise, Sarah's resolve began to wane.

In Genesis 16:2 Sarah went to Abraham and said, "The Lord has prevented me from bearing children. Please go in to my maid; perhaps I will obtain children through her." Sarah's choice and Abraham's compliance resulted in an illegitimate child named Ishmael. He was not the seed through which the chosen nation would come. While Abraham begged God to use Ishmael, God held His ground and told Abraham that though He would bless Ishmael and give him many descendents, Sarah would still bear a child, and he would be the son of promise. (See Gen. 17:17-21.) A few years later Sarah bore Isaac. In spite of her failures, God sent her blessing and used her life to bring history one step closer to the birth of Christ.

Peter too experienced God's amazing mercy during a second-chance miracle. A Galilean fisherman and among the first called to be a disciple, Peter quickly emerged as a leader among the Twelve. As a part of his calling, Peter received a name that means "rock." He was strong, assertive, and memorable. Always mentioned first in lists of the Twelve and singled out for special revelations of Jesus' deity, Peter pledged to follow Jesus to the death. So the Messiah's prophecy that Peter would deny their relationship three times seemed hard to believe. But Peter soon did just that.

After such a fall it seemed Peter's job as a disciple was over. What employer would ever keep a staff member who was disloyal and untrustworthy—much less offer him a promotion within the organization? Certainly he'd not be allowed to have a close intimate relationship with the One he'd just so vehemently denied. Yet a close look at a tender conversation between the resurrected Jesus and the disreputable disciple tells us otherwise. In John 21:15-17 Jesus gave the disciple three chances to reaffirm his commitment—one chance for each of the three times he had denied the Lord. This time Peter passed the test and soon became one of the most influential men in the spread of Christianity.

I can't read the stories of any of those mentioned without feeling my heart strain with gratitude for God's willingness to use us in spite of our slips and failures. Aaron, Sarah, Peter, and Jonah were given a gift available to you and me as well. If you have fallen out of fellowship with God, if you have made decisions that have taken you further down a path of rebellion than you ever thought you'd go, if you're doing what He's asked but only with half-hearted indifference, know that you've not outrun the grasp of His grace or overstepped the boundaries of His mercy.

Though we can't undo past mistakes, we can move past them through God's mercy and grace. He's always ready to forgive us, to set us on our feet, to dust (or dry) us off, and to take our hands as we continue the journey at His side.

Chapter 2
SECOND CHANCES

*God—always the loving parent—rejoices
when His wayward children come home.*

At the end of the last chapter, I had trouble peeling myself away from my keyboard. I could've written for hours! From Genesis to Revelation the Bible bulges with account after merciful account of individuals who'd blown it and yet were offered the clemency that only a compassionate God like ours could give.

Joseph's 10 brothers, for instance, appear in the Book of Genesis as a jealous and conniving brood out to seek revenge on their younger brother. They were tired of living in the shadow of the son born to their father's favored wife. Joseph seemed to enjoy a preferential status highlighted by a brilliant robe. The envy in their hearts roared out of control and burst into flames of violence as his brothers plotted to kill Joseph, but plans changed when some passing merchants agreed to buy him as a slave.

Genesis 39–42 chronicles a sorrowful tale, but the account points to another second-chance miracle I don't want you to miss. The merchants who purchased Joseph sold him in Egypt where he became a slave in the house of a captain of Pharaoh's guard, a man named Potiphar.

Can you imagine the despondency and heartache that must have ripped through his young heart each night? Yet "the LORD was with Joseph" (Gen. 39:2), and he found favor in the eyes of his new master. "Potiphar put him in charge of his household, and he entrusted to his care every-thing he owned" (Gen. 39:4, NIV).

Just when Joseph's situation was looking up, he caught the adulterous eye of Potiphar's lecherous wife. When she demanded that he join her in adultery, Joseph responded with godly character: "How then could I do such a wicked thing and sin against God?" (Gen. 39:9, NIV).

Joseph's fidelity earned him a false accusation followed by a prison cell. Yet, despite past circumstances, he rose to prominence and success within the ranks of the Egyptian nation. Within a few years he held power second only to Pharaoh.

When a famine struck, Joseph administered the grain reserves "for the benefit of the Egyptians, and, indeed for all the people of the world."[1] This famine proved the catalyst to bring us to the story's climax. Joseph's brothers were forced to flee to Egypt in search of food. There they came face-to-face with Joseph and found themselves totally at his mercy. While he was completely aware of their identity, they didn't know him until he chose to reveal himself.

With a rush of tears, Joseph explained that he stood before them as the brother they betrayed. But he focused not on meting out punishment or making them grovel for forgiveness; instead, he credited God with using their actions for good, to position Joseph to save Egypt and their father's descendants from starvation. "It was not you who sent me here," he assured them, "but God." In that one statement he lifted a huge burden of guilt off of his brothers' shoulders.

While Joseph could have had them killed or severely punished for the injustice done to him, he, in a breathtaking act of mercy, "kissed all his brothers" and invited them to live under his provision and protection. In a true picture of the merciful Savior to come, Joseph refrained from anger, abstained from vengeance, and offered that which was not deserved.

Joseph consistently exemplified the words the apostle Peter was to write many centuries later to describe Jesus. "When they hurled their insults at him, he did not retaliate; when he suffered, he made no threats. Instead, he entrusted himself to him who judges justly" (1 Pet. 2:23, NIV).

I'm reminded of the story of a young man in our church. Raised by his grandparents in a rough part of town, Daniel made a series of poor choices while growing up. His life plummeted downward until he shot another youth and was sent to juvenile detention. He dreaded the day he'd turn 18 because on that day he'd appear before a court that would likely send him to jail for the rest of his life. But when the day came and Daniel appeared before the judges, he experienced a miracle.

The grandmother of the boy he'd killed wrote an appeal to the court on his behalf. She asked the judges to extend Daniel a second chance. Shockingly, they set him free. Daniel walks in freedom because a forgiving grandma chose to believe that he could start fresh.

In an act of no less generosity, Joseph granted his brothers forgiveness and reconciliation. They even enjoyed the benefits of their savior's success because of grace. How their savior pictured our Savior. Jesus loves to extend to us that same kind of mind-blowing mercy.

The truly incredible part of divine mercy, however, comes not only in our relief over finding forgiveness and receiving a second chance but also in understanding the Father's elation to offer it.

Only in this one place in Scripture did Jesus tell three parables to make one point. In Luke 15, He was surrounded by the city's scoundrels and its elite. Sinners flanked Him on one side and the

Pharisees and scribes on the other. It must have
been quite a scene that day as the riffraff pressed
in to hear Jesus and the Jewish leaders pressed in
to criticize Him.

The religious leaders couldn't believe Jesus
would allow such common, sinful people to get
so close. The Messiah must have overheard their
grumblings about His choice of company because
He told them about a sheep, a coin, and a son that
all had one thing in common: They were lost and
then joyfully rediscovered.

Jesus wanted everyone to relate to His
stories, so He started with men and boys first with
a tale of a beloved sheep who strayed. Sheep have
a propensity to wander. Any shepherd worth his
salt had to work overtime to keep his precious
flock in check. Yet there always seemed to be one
wandering sheep that slipped the shepherd's care-
ful watch and steered off the beaten path.

What great concern must have been in the
shepherd's heart to cause him to leave his others
behind in search of just that one. While they were

equally important, they were safely in his care. So he went looking for the foolish one that didn't even know the danger it was in. Upon finding the wayward animal, the shepherd rushed to his friends and neighbors: "Rejoice with me, for I have found my sheep which was lost!"

No sooner had Jesus concluded this story than He was on to another one about a coin. No doubt, the women in the group leaned forward in anticipation. "When a Jewish girl married, she began to wear a headband of ten silver coins to signify that she was now a wife. It was the Jewish version of our modern wedding ring, and it would be considered a calamity for her to lose one of those coins."[2]

Jesus told of a woman who had one lost coin. He asked the crowd to consider how a woman in this position would address the situation. Would she just sit back and hope that it turned up on its own? Certainly not! She began an all-out search-and-rescue adventure.

I rarely take off my wedding ring, but on one occasion I did and my young son got hold of it. We left no piece of furniture, rug, or appliance unturned until that ring was safely back where it belonged. Sheer panic melted into sweet relief the moment I placed it back on my finger. I can certainly relate to the woman's desire to invite her friends and neighbors to rejoice with her over the find. What a gift to have returned something precious that you thought was forever lost!

No parable summarizes the overwhelming love and relief God feels to have us return to His side, however, quite like the story of the prodigal son. After the younger son squandered his inheritance and turned his back on his father, he still found himself received with love, joy, and feasting at his homecoming. Though the son cried, "Father, I have sinned against heaven and in your sight; I am no longer worthy to be called your son," his dad welcomed and celebrated his return (Luke 15:21). Why? Because the lost son returned. They could start again.

The message of these parables seemed revolutionary to first-century Jewish minds. Never had they considered a God who would search for the lost. They didn't think He cared that much or that He would expend that much energy on one lost soul.

The people of their world thought it was man's job to seek God and, if anything, God was doing the hiding. How marvelous to know God seeks us and rejoices when we're safely at His side. While these parables certainly speak to those in need of salvation, their message unveils the heart of our servant Savior to seek out, save, and salvage those He loves.

I'm so grateful that God doesn't shelve us but still applauds and even rejoices when we surrender completely to Him. I love that we serve a God who is tender, who has a Father's heart toward us.

My husband Jerry is never more attractive to me than when I see him extend and bestow mercy on our boys. Sometimes when they've done something and know they should "get it," they

29

look nervously up at their daddy who chooses to allow his frustration or disappointment over what they've done to melt into a smile of mercy and grace. While Jerry never excuses their sin or disobedience, he does occasionally make the choice to allow a little mercy to do his talking for him. What a beautiful picture of our Father's love as that big, burly guy extends love and favor to those sweet little boys.

Our God has a Father's compassion. He doesn't look down on us, pointing an accusing finger in our faces. Instead, He sits on the edge of His throne, waiting for our return. How He wants to give us a second opportunity! A second chance to walk with Him.

This ancient biblical record gives us modern-day encouragement: God delights to welcome us back to His side. If you've chosen, like Jonah did, to run from God's will but now you've decided to abandon the pathway of rebellion and yield to the divine interruption He is allowing, then know that your Savior celebrates.

Don't think that your mess-ups make you unfit for service. Rejoice that God extends you grace! Marvel in the fact that He loves you, rejoices over you, and offers you a second chance.

Chapter 3

SHORTCUTS

*The work God is trying to do in you
requires your full participation.*

I'm not the most technologically savvy person, but I have become very adept at texting. In a few seconds, using the tip of my right thumb, I can hash out a message complete with jokes and appropriate slang. I've gotten pretty skillful at the little shortcuts that make words easier to manage and quicker to type. With only 140 characters per Twitter message, I've become masterful at finding short ways to say things.

My fondness for shortening words seeps over into writing. Sometimes sitting at my laptop, books and commentaries strewn around me and writing project before me, I'll hurriedly type "Lol" instead of explaining how funny something was or type "2" instead of writing out the number. I've had to erase, rewrite, and remind myself that shortcuts aren't always best.

After second-chance celebrations, this subject might seem a startling brush with reality—no shortcuts with God. Once we return to God's side, we find ourselves full circle to the place where we have to choose full obedience. While we may want to find the easiest road to complete obedience, our hearts must be set on doing God's will—His way and in its entirety—even if it takes longer than we'd prefer or requires more effort.

Jonah had been disciplined and decided to get on board with God's plan. At the appropriate time, God commanded the fish to release the prophet. Scripture does not say where the fish deposited Jonah, but "it is reasonable to assume that Jonah was right back near Joppa where he started."[3] In Jonah 3:2 God reminded Jonah of the job He'd first assigned him: "Arise, go to Nineveh the great city and proclaim to it the proclamation which I am going to tell you." Jonah must have been startled to realize he was back at square one with the same command he'd fled. For him, there'd be no getting out of God's will, no shortcut to Nineveh. He hadn't gotten a full ride to the shores of Assyria courtesy of the "Big Fish Express." Getting there required full, detailed obedience.

Many scriptural examples show people who tried to take a shortcut to obeying God, and I imagine most of us can relate to the tendency. Saul kept some of the best spoils of the Amalekites instead of destroying everything as God instructed him. The rich young man wanted to achieve salvation by doing everything but what Jesus required. It seems even Satan knows the unbelievably tragic effects taking shortcuts can have because he even tried to get Jesus to take the easy road (Matt. 4).

In 2 Kings we meet Naaman, a man who learned an important lesson about the details of obedience. He was captain of the Syrian army and highly respected for the battles he'd waged and won. You'd think a man in charge of a vast army would appreciate the gravity of meticulously receiving and following instructions, yet he was unwilling to do so himself. Naaman had leprosy. When he learned that a prophet in Samaria might be able to heal him, he took a letter from his king to the king of Israel requesting his help. Elisha was determined to show Naaman that there was a true prophet in Israel (2 Kings 5:8) and that the God of Israel could heal. Elisha gave Naaman specific instructions: "Go and wash in the Jordan seven times, and your flesh will be restored to you and you will be clean" (v. 10).

Naaman was furious. He didn't like what he was told to do, how Elisha told him to do it, or where he was told to carry out the instructions. Naaman's preconceived ideas of how his healing would take place initially kept him from humbly doing what God required. He even suggested a better method to procure his healing (v. 12). He wanted to bathe in the waters of Abanah and Pharpar, rivers located in his hometown. Naaman knew them to be clean and clear compared to the Jordan. He was appalled that someone of his stature would have to dip himself into the Jordan's dirty waters. The Syrian rivers, he felt, would not only be cleaner but more convenient. Like many of us, he preferred to suggest to God "better" ways to accomplish His purposes.

Recently I spoke on Jonah and the interrupted life at a church in Maryland. Afterward, an older woman walked up to me with a solemn face. She seemed overwhelmed and frustrated as she began, "Thanks for your message. I needed to hear it. I raised three children and was looking forward to retirement. I've yet to enjoy it because my daughter has made some bad choices, and I am now raising my four grandchildren. I know it's the right thing and I love them dearly, but I'm often tempted to find another place for them to grow up. I'm frustrated at what God has asked of me for this season of life. It's not what I had in mind."

While I encouraged this sweet grandmother, I understood her concern and could relate to her desire to find another option. This is precisely the way we feel when, like Naaman and this godly woman in Maryland, we meet up with instructions from God that don't fit with what we had in mind or seem to be unnecessarily inopportune.

Our inclination? To find another route to accomplish what God requires that won't take as much effort or energy as we will have to expend to obey God completely. Yet Joppa—the place of decision and the crossroads of obedience—seems to be the starting place of most second chances. It reminds us that God seldom offers shortcuts. He knows we'll grow in the journey, and so He still wants us to take it, all of it, one step at a time.

Naaman's wise servants, people who knew the value of carrying out instructions with precision, encouraged him and eventually caused him to see the futility of trying to circumvent God's directions. What Naaman needed to learn is the same thing we do: Full obedience to the Word is imperative for the full purposes of God to be accomplished in our lives

Consider what Jesus came to do. Through His death on the cross, He made it possible for sinful you and me to enter into relationship with God. But the Lord knew He couldn't accomplish the task by merely declaring Himself in charge.

He had to die as a sacrifice for our sin. While another plan might have seemed easier, it would've failed to accomplish God's purposes or to liberate us. Jesus submitted to the Father's plan for Him with full obedience, even to the point of death. How can we balk when He asks us to partner with Him?

The work God is trying to do in you requires your full participation. You will find the rewards when you subscribe completely to what He asks and do the tasks how and where He asks.

Remember, when Jonah landed back at Joppa, he knew he had to devote himself fully to God's will. No shortcuts could navigate the miles to Nineveh. He had to put one foot in front of the other and trust God for the rest. Now was the time to obey fully, wholeheartedly. Whether Jonah realized it at the time, world change lay on the horizon.

The greatest revival in history happened because one man surrendered to God. How many things hinge on your full obedience?

Chapter 4
MOVING FORWARD

God's presence is with you to guide and empower you to carry out His will.

Last evening was a long one. What should have been a fun day of after school outside playtime followed by a family picnic dinner turned sour when I got the news that one of my sons had been disobedient to his teacher at school. His teacher sent me messages letting me know about a stubborn rebellious streak rearing its ugly head. While I have a tiny inkling about where it came from, the behaviors he'd exhibited were unacceptable.

Instead of enjoying a festive family afternoon, I had to split my time between the two who wanted to continue with our plans and the one who was relegated to the house. There he sat, pouting at the kitchen table. I took out his homework folder and noticed that he had more work than normal. Instead of the few usual math or spelling worksheets, he had accumulated quite a stack.

A note from the teacher explained: "I'm sorry that there is more work than normal. This is not only your son's homework but also the work he refused to do in class today. Thank you for your help."

When I put the familiar worksheets down on the table in front of him, he squirmed at the sight. Seemed like déjà vu.

It was, and then some.

Jonah too may have felt a mild case of déjà vu when God once again instructed him to head to Nineveh. Seems like the same assignment, right? Well yes, but close examination of the passage reveals that God laid a bit more challenge on the table this time around. While the prophet's mission destination was the same, the directives changed a bit. In chapter 1, his instructions were clearer. God implicitly told Jonah what to do on Assyrian soil. Both His message and its purpose were unmistakable. But this time, while Jonah still knew obedience would require a one-way ticket out of town and that he'd need to make a proclamation, he received ambiguous insight on what the message should be. Instead of simply being required to go, he had to move forward without preassembled plans and details. While both commands required obedience, this one necessitated a greater measure of faith. It forced Jonah to rely more heavily on help yet to come. But with these new divine instructions—"go to Nineveh … and proclaim to it the proclamation which I am going to tell you" (3:2)—came a hidden promise that Jonah could count on. God's presence was going with him all the way to Nineveh to give him guidance and strength as he moved forward in obedience.

When we surrender to the divine intervention He allows, we can depend on a Helper for the journey. At the moment we receive Christ, God's Holy Spirit takes up residence in us. In Old Testament days the Holy Spirit would come and go when a specific task was completed or when the person rebelled against God. That's why, in the psalms, we find King David crying out, "Do not cast me away from Your presence" (Ps. 51:11).

The Spirit of God is always with us modern believers. We don't go through life by ourselves. With the Holy Spirit in us, we take the presence of God with us. If today you've been asked to obey God in a specific area where you feel lonely, afraid, or unclear on how to proceed and think you won't have the power, patience, or words to pull off what God's asked you to do, there is good news: You've got God's presence to help you on the journey. He has not left you alone to fend for yourself in the interrupted life. He is with you every step of the way.

One of my favorite passages in all Scripture is John 16. In this chapter, Jesus spoke tenderly with the disciples on the eve of His crucifixion. They were sorrowful because He had explained in no uncertain terms that He would soon leave them and return to the Father. In an effort to calm their emotions, He said that it was advantageous to them for Him to leave. As He walked the earth in human form, Jesus chose to limit His divinity to time and space. His presence, then, could be in only one place at a time. But the gift of the Holy Spirit—a gift who came only after Christ's return to heaven—overcame that limitation. In promising the disciples that the Spirit would come to them, Jesus effectively promised to send them His full and complete presence to help them, to convict them, and to guide them.

When Jerry and I were first married, we traveled to the Holy Land, where we had the most wonderful and knowledgeable tour guide. I was amazed by his explanation at each location. I had my notebook and pen in hand and took a prodigious amount of notes.

At the end of our wonderful 10 days, I thought back over all the places we'd been, glanced at my notes, and felt overwhelmed. I realized then the importance of only receiving information a bit at a time. If our guide had given us a map with the major stops circled and a run-down of each location's significance and then sent us on our way, it would have been a catastrophe. We could never have absorbed it all right then and there.

There were far too many details and directions for us to soak in all at one time. What made the trip so memorable was our interaction with the guide every day and at every site on the tour. Following him from one destination to the next, leaning in and listening to each explanation, and engaging in his wisdom step-by-step made the experience worthwhile. This is what good guidance looks like.

God gave the Spirit to the disciples as an internal compass to help them find their way. They could rest easy in Jesus' departure and the partial information He'd given them—not because they had enough notes from their three years with Him to carry with them through the rest of their lives but because a wise and wonderful Director would lead them with step-by-step instructions. If they'd listen, He'd guide. If they'd follow, He'd lead. The result? Lives well lived and journeys well taken.

You and I have some spiritual miles we need to travel as we surrender to the divine intervention God has for us. The road from your Joppa to the Nineveh God is sending you to will require a divine empowerment that only the Spirit can give. But God can work within you "to will and to work for His good pleasure" (Phil. 2:13). He can guide you, compel you, change you, comfort you, and empower you with His own presence as you choose to surrender to what He's allowed. Through the Holy Spirit He gives us the desire and the ability to live for His glory.

None of us can accomplish much on our own, but if the presence of God is in us and if the power of God is with us, we have every opportunity, every capability, to meet whatever challenge God sets before us.

As you commit to follow the Lord with complete and full obedience, know that you don't need to have all the answers. In His timing, through the power of the Holy Spirit, God will give you directions and then empower you to carry them out.

Chapter 5
MAKING GOOD & MAKING AMENDS

Obedience is better than sacrifice.

"Act first and apologize later" is a motto some people live by. They believe getting their actions approved ahead of time is overrated. They don't ask permission before doing something for fear that they might be told not to do it. So, to get and do what they want, they just move forward and hope for the best. In the end, if they find they have done something wrong, then they just spend time apologizing and making amends. Jonah may have liked this motto, but after a stay in the fish's belly, the prophet was genuinely serious about getting things straight between him and God.

In the second chapter of Jonah, the prophet did more than agree to go to Nineveh. He also agreed to return to the Holy Land. Verse 9 tells us he wanted to "sacrifice to [God] with the voice of thanksgiving." This refers to his desire to return to the Holy Land where he would offer the Lord the proper ritual sacrifice in the temple. The sacrifices and vows Jonah offered to make were not merely signs of gratitude but also served as a visible demonstration of his atonement for his rebellion. In the prophet's day, sacrifices and ceremonies were a mandated necessity for God's people.

I find it interesting that when the prophet was freed from the belly of the fish, Yahweh told him to go not to the temple to make the promised sacrifices but to head to Nineveh first. Jonah's narrative ends before we discover if or when he went to Jerusalem, but we are certain that he didn't go before obeying the original command. Making good by going to Nineveh was more important than making amends by going to Jerusalem.

When we come out of a season of running from God, it can be tempting to try to make reparations for our actions. In a strange way, we sometimes feel like we need to "be good" to compensate for lost time. But I believe God would rather us get right with Him, like Jonah in chapter 2, and then focus on obedience rather than use our energy to first try to make amends to Him for our past disobedience. Psalm 51:16-17 teaches, "[God] You do not delight in sacrifice, otherwise I would give it; You are not pleased with burnt offering. The sacrifices of God are a broken spirit; a broken and a contrite heart, O God, You will not despise." Though sacrifices were essential in Old Testament times, as far as our Father is concerned, obedience is better than sacrifice.

Another compelling illustration of this concept appears in 1 Samuel. The prophet told King Saul the Lord wanted him to lead the children of Israel out against the Amalekites. Samuel told Saul in no uncertain terms to completely annihilate this enemy who had plagued God's people for centuries. God required the death of the king, every person, and even all the animals. The Israelites were to destroy everything and retain no plunder for themselves (1 Sam. 15:3). Saul obediently gathered up an army of 210,000 warriors and headed out to destroy the Amalekites. But rather than wiping out everything as instructed, Saul decided to spare Agag the king as well as the best of the nation's livestock.

Like Jonah, Saul chose his own path instead of yielding completely to the one mapped by God. The Lord knew what Saul had done and told Samuel He regretted making Saul king of the people. When Samuel went to confront him, Saul made no attempt to hide the fact that Israel had taken the best their enemies had to offer. Rather, he sought to make up for his disobedience by using a very compelling excuse.

According to 1 Samuel 15:21 Saul said the goods they'd taken from the land would be used to make sacrifices to the Lord. Saul had foregone obedience and was looking to make amends through his sacrifice.

In Old Testament days Yahweh allowed sacrifices to serve as the atonement for sin, but they were not His ultimate desire. God longed for people who had a heart to obey Him and who would choose to remain in fellowship with Him more than He wanted a people who would choose their own paths and then run to the tabernacle to gain forgiveness for their actions.

Offering sacrifices was easier for King Saul than willing obedience. To obey, he had to deny his own desires and yield to God. Denying the flesh always requires effort. How much easier it seems to repent later than to initially submit.

Obedience, I've found, necessitates self-denial. Subjecting our will to the Lord's is often more difficult than kneeling at an altar and asking for His mercy. Now don't get me wrong, He is willing to extend mercy, but His heart is gladdened and His name glorified when His people desire to obey Him in the first place.

Hear me clearly: The Lord is always willing to forgive. He is quick to extend mercy. If you stand in need of His forgiveness today, then know that He is waiting to pardon you. Yet He desires that the knowledge of His long-suffering way and His willingness to show grace not dissuade you from the higher calling of obedience.

The apostle Paul, speaking of God's boundless grace, wrote: "What shall we say then? Are we to continue in sin that grace may increase? May it never be!" (Rom. 6:1-2). Knowing the endless kindness of our God should not only catapult us to our knees to experience it but to our feet, to walk out a lifestyle of obedience that prioritizes submission to His will over all else.

Whatever God has asked you to do, get to it. Whatever divine intervention He has placed in your path, yield to it. Act on what God asks of you. Our surrender pleases the Father's heart.

CONCLUSION

Interruptions. We equate them with upheaval, derailment, and frustration. But over the years, I've learned to recognize that when God allows interruptions they are often a pathway to His greater purpose.

Imagine that you've prepared a beautiful, candle-lit dinner for your spouse. The house smells wonderful. You've spent all day getting ready. You can't wait to hear that front door open. Suddenly, the phone rings. Thinking a salesman's on the line, you frown and grumble about the interruption. You don't realize, however, that a sweepstakes host waits for you to pick up. In his hands he holds a ten million dollar check made out to you. The ring that you wanted to ignore is, in fact, the ring that would change your life. Suddenly, you have a brand-new perspective on that annoying phone call.

When God allows interruptions in our journeys it is a divine intervention—a chance He is giving you to walk down His path and fulfill the destiny He mapped out for you long ago. It's a call to walk away from your plans and work at His side. It's the grand prize: discovering and engaging in God's will for us. Agreeing to go with Him to Nineveh, no matter how distasteful it may initially appear, will bring blessings we can't imagine.

Prior to the four chapters of the book bearing his name, Jonah is mentioned only by name, hometown, religion, and job title (2 Kings 14:25). But after the prophet was interrupted by God's intervention and chose to surrender to it, he was known for more than just the stats on his résumé. Now he is known throughout the ages as a man who made a mark in history for the Kingdom of God, and it all started with an interruption.

Your life is destined to have an eternal significance, and it will most likely begin on the heels of an interruption. Many Christians spend their years searching for significance. They buy best sellers and pack arenas to hear self-help speakers, all in an attempt to find purpose. To matter. To find the formula for lasting success. Few realize that God's intervention is often the cure-all for the significance search. When we agree to what He asks and surrender to His prescription for our lives, we'll be more than just a name, social security number, or job description. We become a major player in the unfolding of God's Kingdom on planet earth. A spiritual sweepstakes winner. Now that's significant.

Maybe you've decided to yield to God's call to Nineveh but the thought of taking your hands off the steering wheel of life feels a little scary. Maybe it terrifies you to think that the Lord might ask you to give up personal comfort and security to go where He is leading. Your feelings are certainly understandable but completely unnecessary. You can trust the Father's heart.

Reminds me of my son who stood, bat in hand, in front of a new toy he'd gotten for Christmas. It's a machine that catapults baseballs into the air. A motor shoots them, one after the other, out of a tube. When my husband first put it together, our son saw the frequency and velocity of the balls and resigned himself to defeat.

"I'll never be able to hit those balls."

He whined and complained that he couldn't experience any victory with the new game while we tried to convince him to at least give it a whirl. Finally, he stood several yards in front of the machine with a bat in hand, anxiously awaiting the first pitch.

I felt bad for him. He looked so worried, so apprehensive, so unsure. If only he knew what I did. The game had some gears that could be changed to control the speed and timing of each pitch. His father had already tinkered with them, preparing them to match our son's ability.

Our little boy had nothing to worry about. He'd been set up to win. He simply needed to step up to the plate and play the game.

You don't need to worry about what's coming your way. You've been set up to win. When the Lord speaks over your life, separating you unto Himself for His purposes, or allows circumstances to derail you from your original plan, consider it your invitation to step up to the plate. You've been given the opportunity to write a story beyond your expectations, and He doesn't expect you to go it alone. He partners with you. He's gone before you and prepared the pathway for optimum results, and He'll guide you each step of the way.

The results of your obedience can cause a ripple effect that will astound you and everyone around. So much hinges on your decision to go with God and "lean not on your own understanding" (Prov. 3:5, NIV).

God sits on the edge of His throne, ready to do more than we can ask or think (Eph. 3:20). All He desires is our yielding to His plan.

Say yes to that interruption. Take Him up on that second-chance offer.

Onward, modern-day Jonah.

The best is yet to come.

About the Author

Priscilla Shirer is a Bible teacher whose ministry is focused on the expository teaching of the Word of God to women. Her desire is to see women not only know the uncompromising truths of Scripture intellectually but also experience them practically by the power of the Holy Spirit.

She is the author of a handful of books and Bible studies including *Discerning the Voice of God*, and *One in a Million*.

Priscilla is the daughter of pastor, speaker, and well-known author Dr. Tony Evans. She is married to her best friend Jerry and spends her days cleaning up after three fabulous boys: Jackson, Jerry Jr., and Jude. Priscilla's Web site is:

www.goingbeyond.com

ENDNOTES

1. Paul J. Achtemeir, gen. ed., *Harper's Bible Dictionary* (San Francisco, CA: Harper & Row, Publishers, 1985), 507.
2. Warren W. Wiersbe, *The Bible Exposition Commentary*, vol. 1 (Wheaton, IL: Victor Books, 1989), 234.
3. John Walton, *Jonah: Bible Study Commentary* (Grand Rapids, MI: The Zondervan Corporation, 1982), 35.

What do we do when God interrupts our lives?
Many times, like Jonah, we run! This 7- session, DVD-driven Bible study
teaches that what might seem like an interruption is actually God's
invitation to do something bigger than we could ever imagine.

LIFEWAY.COM/PRISCILLASHIRER | 800.458.2772 | LIFEWAY CHRISTIAN STORES

LifeWay | Women